NORTHUMBERLAND TRAVEL GUIDE 2024

"A Journey Through Legends, Landscapes, and Local Life With Images Maps"

SCUTT FURMAN

COPYRIGHT © 2024 by SCUTT FURMAN.

All rights reserved. No part of this publication may be reproduced, distributed, or transmitted in any form or by any means, including photocopying, recording, or other electronic or mechanical methods, without the prior written permission of the publisher, except in the case of brief quotations embodied in critical reviews and certain other noncommercial uses permitted by copyright law.

1| Northumberland Travel Guide 2024

TABLE OF CONTENTS

Introduction **6**
    Welcome to Northumberland 6
    Bringing Northumberland to Light: A Short History ... 7
CHAPTER 1 .... **12**
    Newcastle Upon Tyne - The Vibrant Gateway 12
    The Quayside: Where History Meets Modernity 12
    Nightlife and Gastronomy: Savoring the Geordie Spirit 16
    Must-Visit Museums and Art Galleries 18
    CHAPTER 2 24
    The Enchanting Coastline 24
    Bamburgh Castle: Majestic Fortress by the Sea 24
    Holy Island of Lindisfarne: Spiritual and Mystical ... 27
    Secluded Beaches and Hidden Coves: A Coastal Treasure 30
Chapter 3 .... **34**
    Countryside Charms 34
    The Cheviot Hills: Hiker's Paradise 34
    Kielder Water & Forest Park: Nature's Playground . 36
    Northumberland National Park: Untamed Beauty ... 38
CHAPTER 4 .... **41**
    Historic Towns and Villages 41
    Alnwick: Home to Wizards and Wonder 41
    Hexham: A Fabric of Time 47
    Craster and Seahouses: Seafood and Serenity 50

CHAPTER 5... **53**

    Castles, Keeps, and Ancient Ruins......................... 53

    Alnwick Castle: Where History and Magic Intertwine. 53

    Warkworth Castle: Overlooking the Coquet............55

    Hadrian's Wall: Rome's Northern Frontier.............. 57

CHAPTER 6... **60**

    Unique Experiences...60

    Dark Sky Park: Stargazing in Kielder......................60

    Festivals and Events: Celebrating Northumberland... 62

    Local Legends and Folklore: Tales from the Borders. 65

    Wildlife and Natural Wonders................................. 69

    Farne Islands: A Seabird Spectacle....................... 69

    Red Squirrels and Wild Goats: Wildlife Watching... 72

    Waterfalls and Woodlands: Hidden Natural Gems. 76

CHAPTER 8... **80**

    Where Couples Can Visit...80

    Romantic Beach Walks: Embleton Bay and Beyond.. 80

    Luxurious Getaways: Spa Hotels and Boutique B&Bs...83

    Candlelit Dinners: Top Romantic Restaurants........ 87

CHAPTER 9:.. **92**

    Where Kids Can Visit... 92

    Alnwick Garden: A Wonderland for All Ages.......... 92

    Northumberland Zoo: A Family Adventure............. 95

Bamburgh Beach: Fun and Frolic by the Sea.........99
CHAPTER 10..102
    Travel Tips and Practical Information.................... 102
    Getting Around: Transport Tips.............................102
    Where to Stay: From Luxury to Cozy B&Bs..........106
    Luxury Stays:... 107
    Mid-Range Hotels:... 108
    Local Cuisine: Must-Try Northumbrian Dishes...... 111
CHAPTER 11..115
    Day Trips and Itineraries....................................... 115
    Perfect Weekend in Northumberland..................... 115
    Family-Friendly Adventure..................................... 119
    Romantic Escapes and Hidden Getaways............ 121
CHAPTER 12..124
    Beyond Northumberland... 124
    Excursions to the Scottish Borders........................ 124
    Kelso and Floors Castle: A Scottish Delight.......... 126
    Melrose and Abbotsford: Literary and Historical Riches... 127
    Continuing Your English Adventure....................... 133
    Local Language and Phrases: Talking Like a Local.... 140
CONCLUSION..143

5| Northumberland Travel Guide 2024

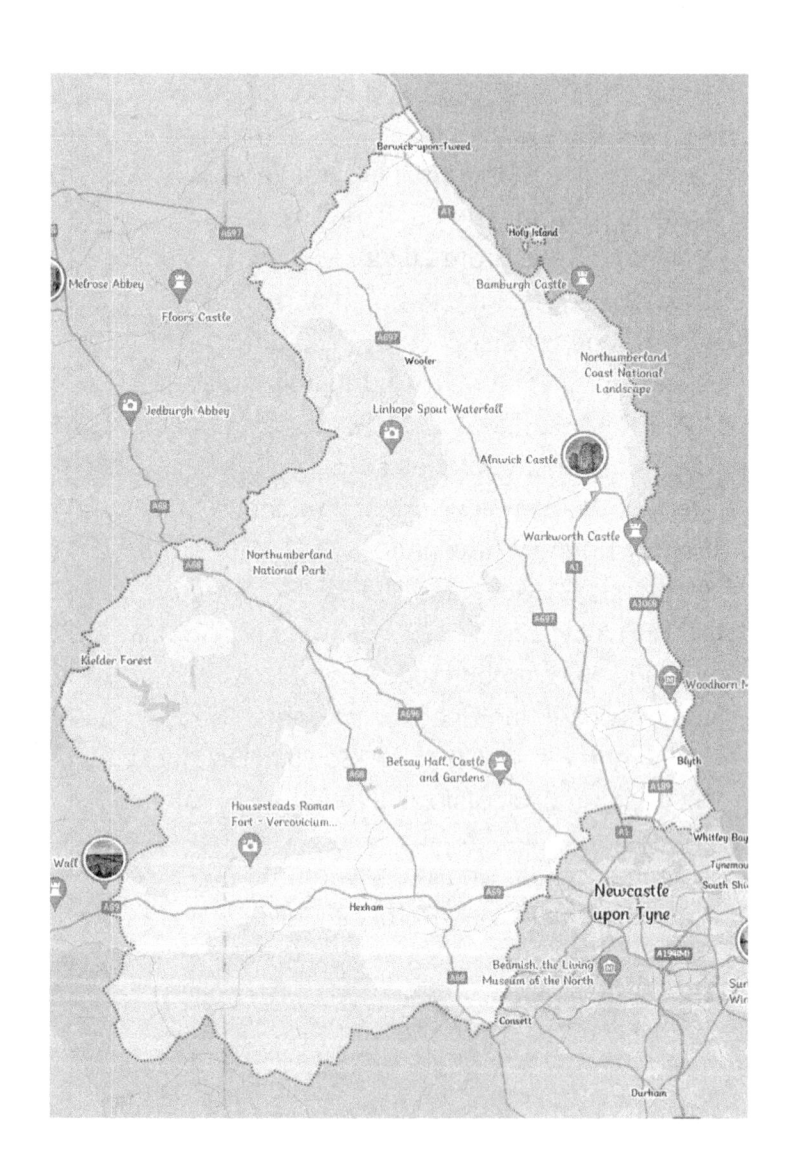

Introduction

Welcome to Northumberland

Hello and welcome to Northumberland, a beautiful place where the past and the present come together in the most interesting ways.

While traveling through this interesting area, you'll come across a scenery that is full of old war stories and buildings that have stood the test of time. Northumberland's rough beauty, from its rocky beaches to its peaceful farmland, draws in families, couples, and people on adventures alike. So, get your guide and get ready to learn about England's northern gem and its beauty.

Bringing Northumberland to Light: *A Short History*

The Land of Stories

Picture yourself standing on the old ground where every rock and river has a story to tell. Northumberland is more than just a place to visit; it's like a tale come to life. This land has been the setting for many stories and important events in history.

Long before the lines were made, the land was home to the Votadini group, whose fighters roamed the hills and rivers. These early people lived in peace with the land, and their tales of bravery and resilience passed down through generations. The memories of their lives can still be felt today, especially when visiting the remains of their villages spread across the countryside.

With the coming of the Romans, Northumberland's story took on new dimensions. The building of Hadrian's Wall, an enormous Roman fortress, was more than just a barrier; it was a show of power and determination. Stretching 73 miles across the northern border, the wall stands as a testament to Rome's ambition and building skill. Walking along its ancient stones, one can't help but imagine the armies of soldiers who once walked its length, guarding the empire's edge against the strange tribes beyond.

Castles, Battles, and Borderlands

Northumberland's strategic situation made it a focus point of war and conquering. The countryside is dotted with castles, each with its own story of defense and power. Alnwick Castle, for instance, rises magnificently from the rolling hills, its stone walls having watched centuries of turmoil and victory. Once a fearsome castle, today it serves as a view into the medieval past, allowing tourists to step back in time and tour its grand rooms and lush grounds.

Bamburgh Castle, set high on a rocky hilltop facing the North Sea, offers another glimpse into the region's fighting past. As you stand on its battlements, the salty sea breeze in your face, it's easy to see why this site was picked for defense. The castle has seen countless fights, from Viking attacks to the Wars of the Roses, each leaving its mark on the strong stone walls.

The steady state of fighting between England and Scotland made a unique character for Northumberland, forming its culture and people. Towns like Berwick-upon-Tweed changed hands so many times that the very idea of the country became fluid. This history of war has left a legacy of strong communities, proud of their roots and the scars that tell their stories.

But Northumberland isn't just about old strife; it's also a land of peace and stunning beauty. The rolling Cheviot Hills, with their soft slopes and vast views, offer a peaceful backdrop to the excitement of the coast. Here, you can hike along paths worn by generations, where every turn shows a new view more stunning than the last.

As you discover Northumberland, you'll find that every castle, hill, and shore has a story to tell. Whether it's the ancient words of the Votadini, the imposing presence of Roman troops, or the sounds of medieval knights, this area is a live fabric of history and fantasy. Welcome to Northumberland, where the past is always present and every trip is a step back in time.

CHAPTER 1

Newcastle Upon Tyne - The Vibrant Gateway

Welcome to Newcastle Upon Tyne, the lively heart of Northumberland, where the rich history of the past meets the powerful pulse of the present. Whether you're walking the historic Quayside, indulging in the local nightlife, or visiting the city's cultural institutions, Newcastle offers a great introduction to the wonders of Northumberland.

The Quayside: *Where History Meets Modernity*

Walking along the Quayside is like stepping into a live museum. Here, you'll find a mix of historic buildings and modern wonders that perfectly capture Newcastle's spirit.

Highlights:

- **Tyne Bridge**: Iconic and historic, linking Newcastle and Gateshead.

- **Millennium Bridge**: Known as the "Blinking Eye Bridge," this walking and bike bridge tilts to allow boats to pass underneath.
    - **Address**: S Shore Rd, Gateshead NE8 3AE
    - **Cost**: Free

- **Personal Experience:** Walking across the Millennium Bridge at sunset is a unique experience. As the bridge lights up, it offers a beautiful view of the river and skyline.

- **Bessie Surtees House:** A pair of 16th and 17th-century trade houses where you can tour beautifully kept rooms.
  - **- Address**: 41-44 Sandhill, Newcastle upon Tyne NE1 3JF
  - **- Cost**: Free

- **Personal Experience:** Stepping inside Bessie Surtees House feels like moving back in time. The shifting wooden floors and historical objects give a real sense of life in Newcastle centuries ago.

- **Quayside Market:** Held every Sunday, this market offers a mix of local crafts, food, and antiques.
    - **Address**: Quayside, Newcastle upon Tyne NE1 3DE
    - **Cost:** Free to look; things priced individually
    - **Personal Experience:** The Quayside Market is a must-visit. I found unique handmade jewelry and enjoyed some delicious street food while soaking in the lively atmosphere.

Nightlife and Gastronomy: *Savoring the Geordie Spirit*

Newcastle's nightlife is known for its variety and energy. Whether you prefer traditional pubs, chic drink bars, or fine eating, Newcastle has something to offer.

Highlights:

- **The Botanist:** A unique bar with a garden-like setting and amazing views.
  - **Address:** Monument Mall, Newcastle upon Tyne NE1 5AU
  - **Cost:** Cocktails from £8-£12
  - **Personal Experience:** The rooftop deck at The Botanist offers great views over the city. The quirky decor and original drinks make it a great spot for an evening out.

- **The Crown Posada:** One of Newcastle's oldest pubs, known for its traditional decor and great drinks.
    - **Address:** 31 The Side, Newcastle upon Tyne NE1 3JE
    - **Cost:** Pints from £4-£6
    - **Personal Experience**: The Crown Posada's stained-glass windows and Victorian furnishings take you to another age. It's a nice place to enjoy a pint and chat with the friendly locals.

- **House of Tides**: A Michelin-starred restaurant offering a changing tasting menu.
    - **Address**: 28-30 Close, Newcastle upon Tyne NE1 3RF
    - **Cost**: Tasting meal from £95 per person
    - **Personal Experience:** Dining at House of Tides was a culinary treat. Each course was a work of art, showing the best of local and

seasonal products. The ancient building added to the charm of the experience.

- **Fat Hippo Underground:** Famous for its indulgent burgers and relaxed atmosphere.
  - **Address**: 2-6 Shakespeare St, Newcastle upon Tyne NE1 6AQ
  - **Cost**: Burgers from £9-£15
  - **Personal Experience:** The burgers at Fat Hippo Underground are the best I've ever had. Juicy, delicious, and served with large amounts of sides, it's a great spot for a relaxing meal.

Must-Visit Museums and Art Galleries

Newcastle is home to an array of museums and galleries that offer something for everyone, from history buffs to art fans.

Highlights:

- Great North Museum: Hancock: Features shows on natural history, archaeology, and world cultures.

- **Address:** Barras Bridge, Newcastle upon Tyne NE2 4PT

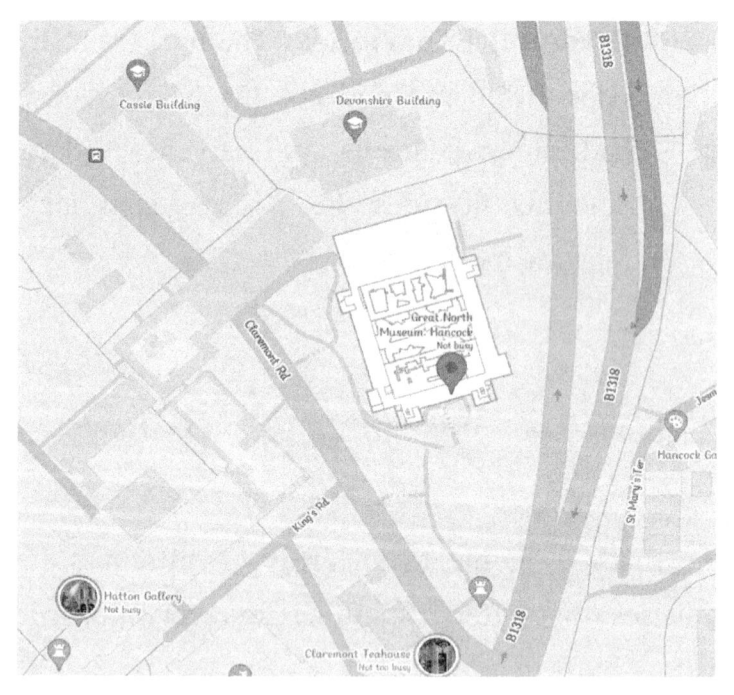

- **Cost**: Free
- **Personal Experience:** The life-size T. rex skull at the Great North Museum was a hit with my kids. The engaging shows kept them occupied for hours.

- **Laing Art Gallery:** Houses a collection of British oil paintings, drawings, ceramics, and modern art.

- **Address:** New Bridge St, Newcastle upon Tyne NE1 8AG
- **Cost**: Free, donations appreciated
- **Personal Experience**: The Laing Art Gallery's collection of John Martin's dramatic scenery was fascinating. The calm mood makes it a perfect place to relax and admire art.

- **Baltic Centre for Contemporary Art**: Located in a converted flour mill, this gallery shows cutting-edge modern art.

- **Address**: S Shore Rd, Gateshead NE8 3BA
- **Cost**: Free, donations appreciated
- **Personal Experience**: The Baltic Centre's ever-changing exhibitions are always thought-provoking. The sweeping views from the top floor are worth the visit alone.

In Newcastle Upon Tyne, history, technology, and culture mix to create a city that's both vibrant and deeply rooted in its past. From the historic Quayside to the lively nightlife and rich cultural offers, Newcastle serves as the perfect entrance to the wonders of Northumberland. Enjoy the friendliness of the Geordie spirit, taste local flavors, and immerse yourself in the various experiences this city has to offer.

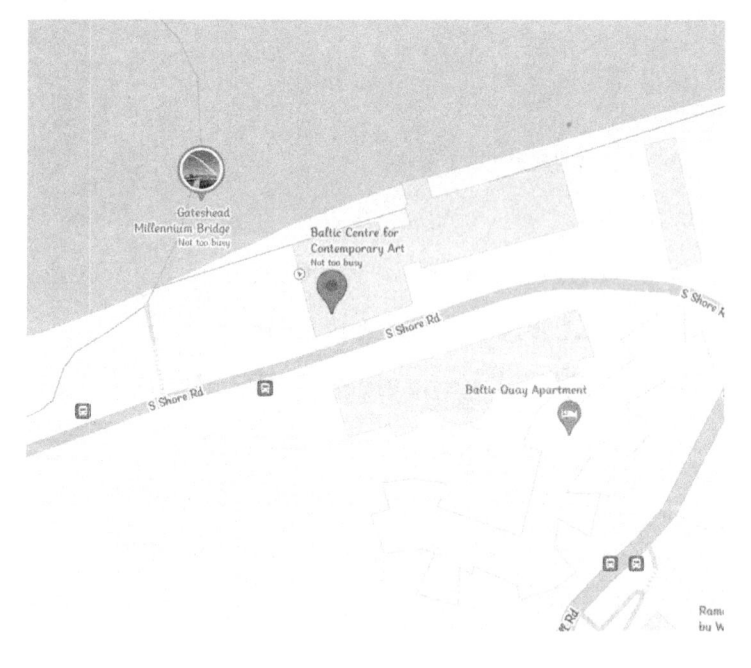

CHAPTER 2

The Enchanting Coastline

Northumberland's shoreline is nothing short of beautiful, where tall castles overlook wild beaches and secret coves invite exploration. From the towering glory of Bamburgh Castle to the spiritual aura of Holy Island, this chapter will guide you through some of the most charming seaside sites in Northumberland.

Bamburgh Castle: *Majestic Fortress by the Sea*

Bamburgh Castle stands strongly on a basalt crag, its huge stone walls and towers rising sharply above the North Sea. This famous fortress, with a history spanning over 1,400 years, is one of the most beautiful and historically rich castles in England.

Highlights:
- **History and Architecture:** tour the vast history of the castle, from its beginnings as a Celtic fort to its role in the Anglo-Saxon and Norman times. The amazing building reflects various times, each adding to the castle's grandeur.
- **Armoury and State Rooms:** The castle's museum and state rooms house an interesting collection of guns and armor, as well as period furniture and artwork.
- **The King's Hall:** A grand hall with a stunning hammer-beam ceiling, where you can imagine the big feasts and important talks that once took place here.

Visitor Information:
- **Address**: Bamburgh Castle, Bamburgh, Northumberland NE69 7DF

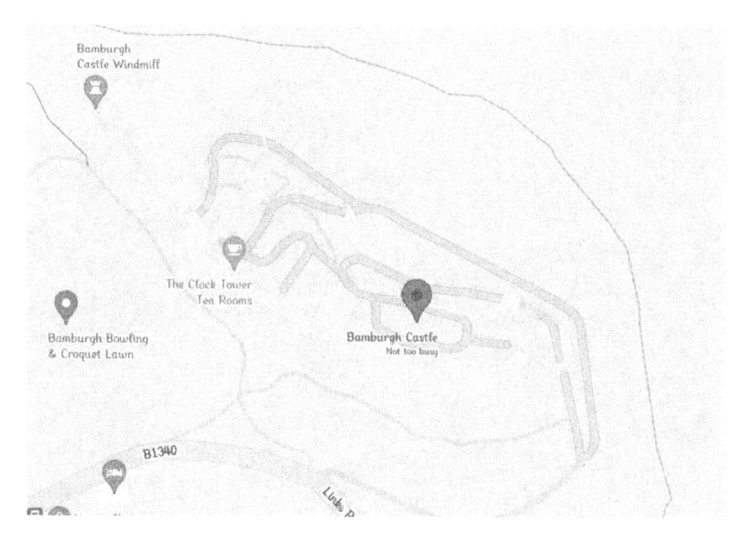

- **Cost**: Adults £14.10, Children £6.95, Family £35.95
- **Personal Experience**: As you walk through Bamburgh Castle, you can almost hear the sounds of heroes and nobles who once walked these rooms. The views from the battlements are simply spectacular, giving wide panoramas of the shoreline and the Farne Islands.

Holy Island of Lindisfarne: *Spiritual and Mystical*

The Holy Island of Lindisfarne, reachable only at low tide via a bridge, is a place of deep peace and historical importance. Known for its early Christian history, Lindisfarne is often referred to as the "Cradle of Christianity" in England.

Highlights:

- **Lindisfarne Priory**: The remains of this early medieval priory are strangely beautiful. Established in the 7th century, it played a key role in the spread of Christianity.

- **Lindisfarne Castle**: Perched on a rocky hill, this beautiful castle offers stunning views and a glimpse into the island's turbulent past.

- **St. Aidan's Winery:** Famous for making Lindisfarne Mead, a delicious honey-based wine. Don't miss the taste events.

Visitor Information:

- **Address**: Holy Island, Berwick-upon-Tweed TD15 2RX
- **Cost**: Free to visit the island; entry fees for Lindisfarne Priory and Castle: Priory Adults £8.00, Children £4.80; Castle Adults £9.00, Children £4.50
- **Personal Experience:** Timing your visit with the waves adds an air of excitement.

Walking the bridge as the sea retreats feels like a journey. The calm of the priory ruins, mixed with the raw beauty of the island, makes for a unique experience.

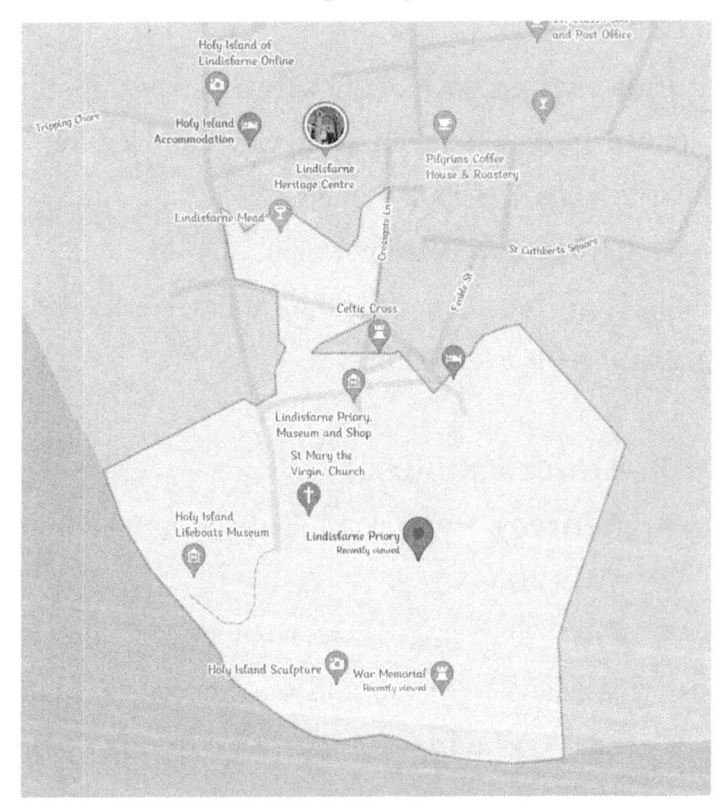

Secluded Beaches and Hidden Coves: *A Coastal Treasure*

Northumberland's shore is dotted with clean beaches and secret bays, perfect for those wanting peace away from the crowds. Here are some of the must-visit spots:

Highlights:

- **Embleton Bay**: This long stretch of golden sand offers beautiful views of Dunstanburgh Castle in the distance. It's great for a peaceful walk or a quiet lunch.
  - **Address**: Embleton, Alnwick NE66 3DT
  - **Cost**: Free
  - **Personal Experience**: The walk from Embleton Bay to Dunstanburgh Castle is beautiful, especially at sunrise. The castle ruins silhouetted against the morning sky create a scene straight out of a fairy tale.

- **Cove Harbour**: A beautiful and lesser-known spot, ideal for those looking to avoid the beaten path. The protected bay is great for a quiet day by the sea.

- **Address:** Near Cocklawburn Beach, Berwick-upon-Tweed TD15 2SR
- **Cost:** Free
- **Personal Experience:** Discovering Cove Harbour felt like finding a secret gem. The solitude and beauty of the cove, mixed with the sound of waves slowly lapping against

the shore, offered a perfect escape from the world.

- **Ross Back Sands:** A private beach available via a beautiful walk through dunes. This pristine beach offers beautiful views of Holy Island and Bamburgh Castle.

- Address: Near Ross Farm, Bamburgh NE70 7EN

- **Cost**: Free
- **Personal Experience:** Ross Back Sands is a secret paradise. The walk to the beach is a bit of an adventure, but the prize is a clean stretch of sand and sea, often with not another soul in sight. It's a great place for a peaceful walk or a lovely evening.

Northumberland's shoreline offers a perfect mix of natural beauty, historical mystery, and quiet escapes. Whether you're visiting the majestic Bamburgh Castle, taking in the spiritual atmosphere of Holy Island, or finding hidden beaches, the charming shore of Northumberland offers a journey filled with awe and wonder.

Chapter 3

Countryside Charms

Northumberland's scenery is a mix of rising hills, thick woods, and quiet scenes that offer an escape into nature's embrace. From the rocky trails of the Cheviot Hills to the vast Kielder Water & Forest Park and the unspoiled beauty of Northumberland National Park, the countryside is a haven for outdoor fans and nature lovers alike.

The Cheviot Hills: *Hiker's Paradise*

The Cheviot Hills, part of the Pennine Way, are a hiker's dream with their wide views, difficult trails, and diverse wildlife. These hills form a natural border between England and Scotland, giving some of the most stunning scenery in Northumberland.

Highlights:

- **Cheviot Summit**: At 815 meters, The Cheviot is the highest point in Northumberland. The hike to the top is difficult but rewards you with panoramic views of the nearby farmland.

- **Hen Hole**: A dramatic valley on the northern hills of The Cheviot, known for its rocky beauty and flowing waterfalls.

- **St. Cuthbert's Way:** A long-distance trail that crosses the Cheviot Hills, giving a mix of historical places and natural beauty.

Visitor Information:

- **Starting Point:** Most hikes start from Wooler, a lovely market town.
- **Address**: Wooler, Northumberland NE71 6LD
- **Cost**: Free; some parking areas may have a fee (usually around £3-£5 per day)
- **Personal Experience**: Hiking up The Cheviot is a thrilling adventure. The scenery

can be difficult, but reaching the top on a clear day, where you can see as far as the North Sea, is incredibly gratifying. Don't forget to pack a good pair of boots and plenty of water.

Kielder Water & Forest Park: *Nature's Playground*

Kielder Water & Forest Park is an outdoor enthusiast's playground, offering a wide range of activities amidst beautiful natural surroundings. The park is home to the biggest man-made lake in Northern Europe and the largest working forest in England.

Highlights:
- **Kielder Water:** Perfect for water sports such as sailing, kayaking, and fishing. The water paths are great for riding and walking.

- **Kielder Observatory**: A dark sky refuge that offers one of the best viewing experiences in the UK.

- **Forest paths:** Over 600 square kilometers of forest with various walking, riding, and mountain biking paths.

Visitor Information:
- **Address:** Kielder Water & Forest Park, Northumberland NE48 1ER
- **Cost:** Varies by exercise; Kielder Observatory tickets: Adults £18, Children £5; Parking: £5 per day
- **Personal Experience:** The peace and calm of Kielder Water are unmatched. Kayaking on the still waters as the forest envelops you is both peaceful and exciting. A visit to the Kielder Observatory on a clear night is a wonderful experience, where the vastness of the world spreads before your eyes.

Northumberland National Park: *Untamed Beauty*

Northumberland National Park is a haven of wild beauty, running from Hadrian's Wall to the Scottish border. It includes various scenery, from rolling hills and river bottoms to vast moorlands and ancient forests.

Highlights:
- **Hadrian's Wall:** A UNESCO World Heritage Site, giving a glimpse into Roman history amidst beautiful scenery.
- **Simonside Hills**: Known for their unique rocky hills and sweeping views, great for climbing.
- **Otterburn Ranges:** A remote and wild place used for military training but available to the public at certain times.

Visitor Information:

- **Address**: Northumberland National Park, Hexham NE46 1BS

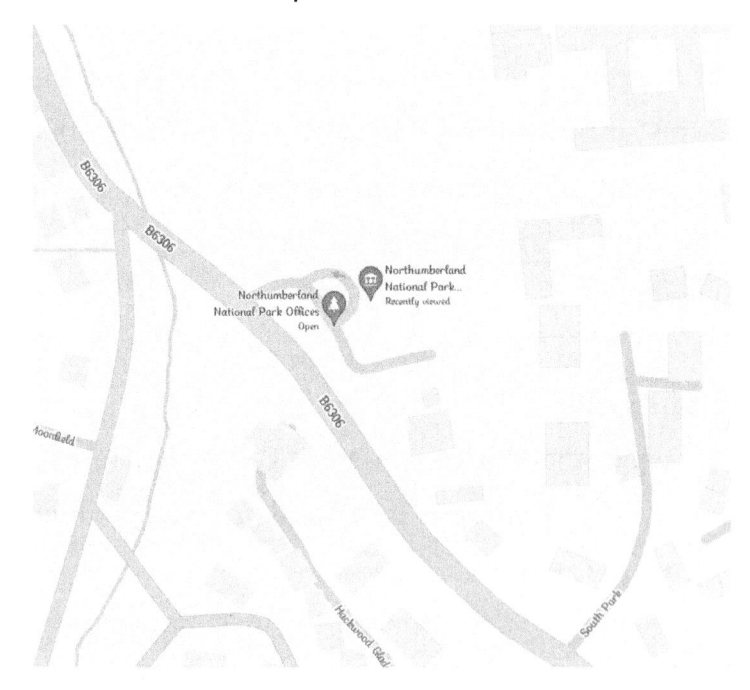

- **Cost**: Free entry; some sites like Housesteads Roman Fort (part of Hadrian's Wall) have an entry fee: Adults £9.90, Children £6.00.

- **Personal Experience:** Exploring Hadrian's Wall was a highlight of my trip. Walking along the old stones, with the vast length of the farmland stretching out on either side, felt like stepping back in time. The rocky beauty of the Simonside Hills provided a great background for a difficult hike, and the sense of solitude was both humbling and thrilling.

Northumberland's farmland charms lie in its natural beauty and various outdoor activities. Whether you're climbing the difficult trails of the Cheviot Hills, enjoying water sports at Kielder Water, or visiting the historical places within Northumberland National Park, each experience offers a unique way to connect with the land and its past. Embrace the beauty and calm of Northumberland's scenery and make memories that will last a lifetime.

CHAPTER 4

Historic Towns and Villages

Northumberland is home to numerous towns and villages, each with its own unique charm and rich past. From the charming market town of Alnwick to the ancient streets of Hexham, and the seaside calm of Craster and Seahouses, these places offer a fascinating glimpse into the region's past and present.

Alnwick: *Home to Wizards and Wonder*

Alnwick is a lovely market town known for its ancient castle, beautiful grounds, and literary links. Steeped in history and filled with character, Alnwick is a must-visit for anyone visiting Northumberland

Highlights:

- **Alnwick Castle:** Known as the "Windsor of the North," this castle has served as a home for the Percy family for over 700 years. It is also famous for its part as Hogwarts in the Harry Potter flicks.

- **Address**: Alnwick Castle, Alnwick NE66 1NQ
- **Cost**: Adults £19.50, Children £10.25, Family £49.50
- **Personal Experience**: Wandering through Alnwick Castle feels like stepping into a tale. The grandeur of the staterooms and the ancient building are awe-inspiring. For

Harry Potter fans, standing on the same grounds where magicians once trained their powers is pure magic.

- **Alnwick Park:** A modern park containing the Grand Cascade, a Poison Garden, and the world's biggest treehouse restaurant.

- **Address:** The Alnwick Garden, Denwick Lane, Alnwick NE66 1YU
- **Cost:** Adults £14.30, Children £6.05, Family £37.50
- **Personal Experience:** The Alnwick Garden is a feast for the senses. The Grand Cascade's falling waters are mesmerizing, and the Poison Garden is both educational and exciting. Dining in the treehouse restaurant, hanging among the trees, is a unique and lovely experience.

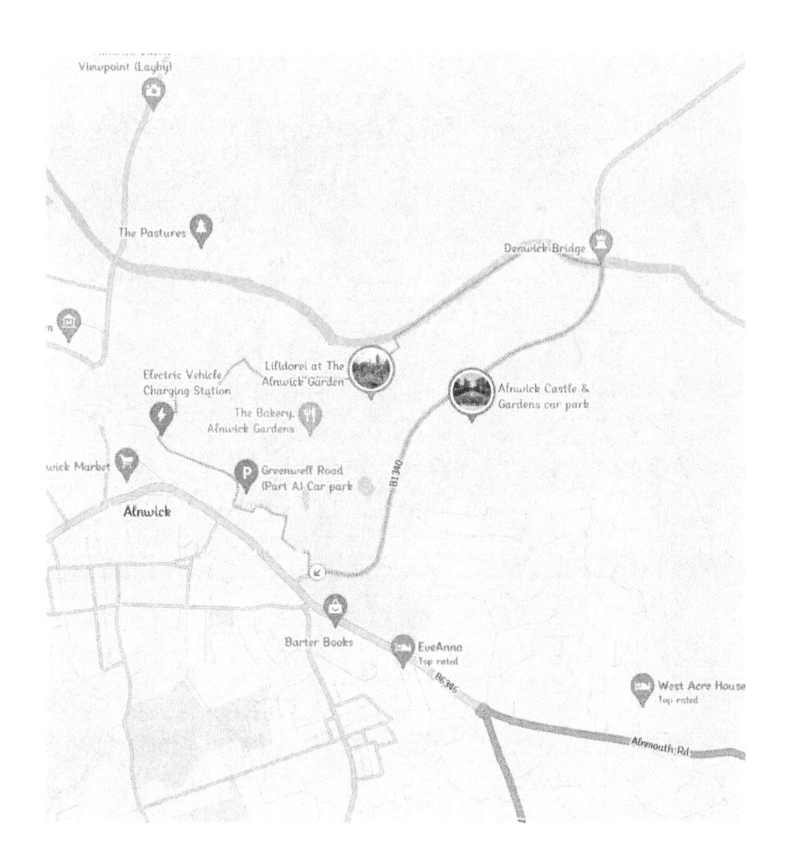

Barter Books: One of the biggest second-hand shops in Europe, based in a converted Victorian train station.

- **Address**: Barter Books, Alnwick Station, Wagon Way Road, Alnwick NE66 2NP
- **Cost**: Free to enter
- **Personal Experience:** Barter Books is a haven for book fans. The cozy nooks and crannies, roaring fires, and endless rows of

books create a wonderfully retro atmosphere. It's easy to lose track of time looking through the unusual collection.

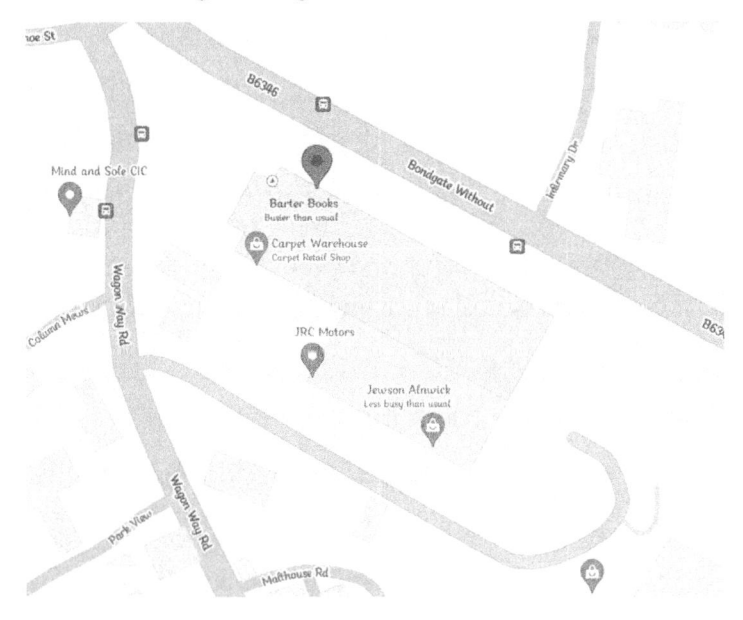

Hexham: *A Fabric of Time*

Hexham is a famous market town with a rich mix of history, from its old abbey to its medieval jail.

Nestled in the Tyne Valley, Hexham offers a mix of beautiful charm and interesting history.

Highlights:

- **Hexham Abbey:** A stunning example of an early English Gothic building, the abbey goes back to the 7th century and houses the beautiful Frith Stool and Night Stair.

- **Address**: Beaumont Street, Hexham NE46 3NB
- **Cost**: Free (donations accepted)
- **Personal Experience:** Hexham Abbey is a place of calm and thought. The elaborate stonework and stained glass windows are fascinating, and the sense of history within the old walls is obvious.

- **Hexham Old Gaol:** England's oldest purpose-built jail, now a museum showing the town's turbulent past.

- **Address:** Hallgate, Hexham NE46 1XD

- **Cost**: Adults £5.00, Children £3.00
- Personal Experience: Visiting Hexham Old Gaol was both scary and interesting. The displays on medieval crime and punishment are well-curated, and the chance to descend into the dark cell offers a chilling glimpse into the past.

Hexham Market Place: The heart of the town, with its old Moot Hall and charming weekly market.

- **Address:** Market Place, Hexham NE46 3PB
- **Cost**: Free
- **Personal Experience**: The Hexham Market Place is busy with action, especially on market days. The mix of local produce, crafts, and street food stalls creates a lively and welcoming atmosphere. Exploring the market is a great way to soak in the local culture.

Craster and Seahouses: *Seafood and Serenity*

Craster and Seahouses are beautiful coastal towns known for their stunning scenery, fresh fish, and relaxed pace of life. These towns are great for those looking to experience the quiet beauty of Northumberland's shore.

Highlights:

- **Craster Harbour:** Famous for its smoked kippers, Craster Harbour is a quaint fishing town with stunning seaside views.
  - **Address:** Craster, Alnwick NE66 3TR
  - **Cost**: Free
  - **Personal Experience:** Strolling around Craster Harbour, the smell of smoked fish wafts through the air. Visiting the neighborhood smokehouse and trying the kippers is a must. The walk to Dunstanburgh

Castle from Craster offers amazing ocean views.

- Dunstanburgh Castle: A dramatic ruin perched on the rocks, reachable via a scenic coastal walk from Craster.
- **Address**: Near Craster, Alnwick NE66 3TT
- **Cost**: Adults £7.00, Children £4.20
- **Personal Experience:** The walk to Dunstanburgh Castle is one of my best hikes. The road runs along the rocky shoreline, with the castle ruins looming in the distance. It's a great spot for photos and camping.

Seahouses Harbour: A busy fishing town known for its boat trips to the Farne Islands and fresh seafood restaurants.
- Address: Seahouses, Northumberland NE68 7RN
- Cost: Free, boat trips to Farne Islands: Adults £20-£40, Children £12-£20

- Personal Experience: Seahouses Harbour is busy and lovely. Taking a boat trip to the Farne Islands to see the puffins and seals was a highlight of my stay. Afterward, indulging in fresh fish and chips at one of the local places was the right end to the day.

Northumberland's historic towns and villages offer a rich mix of experiences, from the charming appeal of Alnwick to the historical depth of Hexham, and the seaside calm of Craster and Seahouses. Each site provides a unique glimpse into the region's past and present, asking you to tour, find, and enjoy the unchanging charm of Northumberland.

53| Northumberland Travel Guide 2024

CHAPTER 5

Castles, Keeps, and Ancient Ruins

Northumberland is a treasure trove of castles, keeps, and old ruins, each telling tales of power, war, and romance. From the stately Alnwick Castle, rooted in both history and magic, to the massive Warkworth Castle and the ancient remains of Hadrian's Wall, these sites provide a captivating journey through time.

Alnwick Castle: *Where History and Magic Intertwine*

Alnwick Castle, often referred to as the "Windsor of the North," is not just a historical fortress but also a place where magic comes alive. Serving as the home of the Percy family for over 700 years, Alnwick Castle has also gained fame as a shooting spot for the Harry Potter series, among other projects.

Highlights:

- **Historical Significance:** Discover the rich history of the castle, from its medieval beginnings to its present role as the home of the Duke of Northumberland.

- **Harry Potter Connection:** Tour the areas used in the Harry Potter films, including the gardens and fields where Hogwarts' flying lessons were made.

- **Art and Architecture:** Marvel at the state rooms filled with an amazing collection of art and artifacts, representing the grandeur of the Percy family's legacy.

Visitor Information:
- **Address**: Alnwick Castle, Alnwick NE66 1NQ

- **Cost**: Adults £19.50, Children £10.25, Family £49.50
- **Personal Experience**: Walking through Alnwick Castle, I was struck by the perfect mix of history and fiction. The state rooms are stunning, adorned with fine art and rich furniture. For Harry Potter fans, the flying training lessons on the very grounds where the scenes were shot is a magical experience that takes you straight into the wizarding world.

Warkworth Castle: *Overlooking the Coquet*

Perched above the River Coquet, Warkworth Castle is a powerful medieval castle with a rich and famous past. Once the center of the powerful Percy family, the castle's impressive keep and vast ruins offer a glimpse into its chaotic past.

Highlights:

- **The Great Tower:** Climb to the top of the keep for stunning views of the nearby scenery and the beautiful village of Warkworth.

- **Chapel and Hermitage:** Visit the nearby Hermitage, a private religious haven cut directly into the rock, reachable by a short boat ride along the River Coquet.

- **Interactive Exhibits:** The castle features educational exhibits that bring its past to life, from the medieval era to its role in the Wars of the Roses.

Visitor Information:

- **Address:** Castle Terrace, Warkworth NE65 0UJ
- **Cost:** Adults £8.90, Children £5.30
- **Personal Experience:** Exploring Warkworth Castle felt like stepping into a medieval journey. The climb to the top of the Great Tower was well worth it for the

sweeping views. The Hermitage, reached by a tranquil boat ride, was a quiet and interesting side trip, adding to the sense of historical discovery.

Hadrian's Wall: *Rome's Northern Frontier*

Stretching across the rocky scenery of northern England, Hadrian's Wall is a colossal relic of Roman Britain. This ancient fortification, built by order of Emperor Hadrian in AD 122, once marked the northernmost boundary of the Roman Empire and remains a testament to Roman engineering and military power.

Highlights:
- **Housesteads Roman Fort:** One of the best-preserved forts along the wall, giving insights into Roman military life with well-preserved barracks, a hospital, and latrines.

- **Sycamore Gap:** A beautiful spot along the wall, showing a single tree made famous by the film "Robin Hood: Prince of Thieves."
- **Vindolanda:** An active historical site and museum, showing amazing finds such as wooden tablets, leather goods, and Roman items.

Visitor Information:
- **Address:** Housesteads Fort, Haydon Bridge, Hexham NE47 6NN

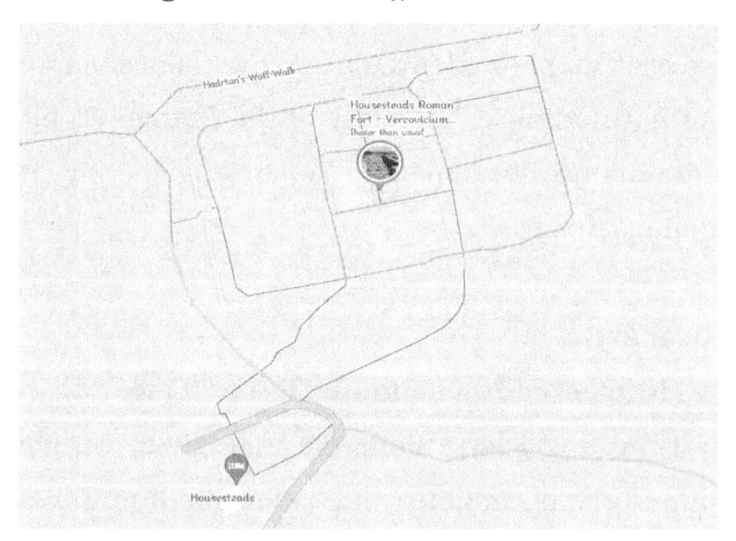

- **Cost**: Adults £9.90, Children £6.00

- **Personal Experience**: Walking along Hadrian's Wall is a remarkable experience. The scale and aspirations of the Romans become obvious as you cross the difficult landscape. Housesteads Fort gives a lively glimpse into the daily lives of Roman soldiers. The walk to Sycamore Gap is both beautiful and quiet, offering a perfect mix of natural beauty and historical mystery. Vindolanda's ongoing digs add a lively element, showing new parts of Roman life with every visit.

Exploring Northumberland's castles, keeps, and old ruins offers a trip through centuries of history. From the magical appeal of Alnwick Castle to the commanding presence of Warkworth Castle and the lasting memory of Hadrian's Wall, these places invite you to step back in time and experience the grandeur and mystery of Northumberland's past.

CHAPTER 6

Unique Experiences

Northumberland is a land of extraordinary experiences, where you can gaze at the stars in a world-renowned dark sky park, join in lively local events, and dig into the rich weave of myths and tales. This part will take you through these unique aspects of Northumberland, ensuring your visit is filled with amazing moments.

Dark Sky Park: *Stargazing in Kielder*

Kielder Water & Forest Park is not only a haven for outdoor sports but also one of the best places in the UK for stargazing. Designated as a Dark Sky Park, Kielder gives a unique chance to experience the beauty of the night sky in one of the darkest places in England.

Highlights:

- **Kielder Observatory**: Nestled in the heart of the park, this observatory offers state-of-the-art telescopes and expert-led events, making it the perfect place to study the stars.

- **Dark Sky Events:** Regular events and classes, including astronomy lessons, astrophotography workshops, and stargazing nights.

- **Milky Way Views:** On bright nights, the Milky Way is visible to the human eye, along with endless stars, planets, and cosmic events.

Visitor Information:

- **Address:** Kielder Observatory, Kielder Water & Forest Park, Northumberland NE48 1ER
- **Cost:** Observatory tickets: Adults £18, Children £5

- **Personal Experience:** Visiting Kielder Observatory was a truly magical event. The sky, free from light pollution, was a stunning painting of stars. The experienced staff took us through the stars, and watching Saturn's rings through a powerful telescope was a highlight. It's a humble and awe-inspiring event that reconnects you with the vastness of the world.

Festivals and Events: *Celebrating Northumberland*

Northumberland's rich cultural heritage is celebrated through a variety of fairs and events that showcase the region's music, arts, history, and customs. These events provide a lively and full experience of local life.

Highlights:

- **Alnwick International Music Festival:** Held every summer, this event features artists from around the world, bringing a wide mix of music and dance to the ancient town.

- **Address**: Various sites in Alnwick, Northumberland NE66
- **Cost**: Free and paid events
- Personal Experience: The Alnwick International Music Festival is a happy celebration of world cultures. The town

comes alive with bright parades, lively acts, and a festive atmosphere. It's a wonderful way to experience Alnwick's community energy and world links.

- Berwick Film & Media Arts Festival: An yearly event that turns the ancient town of Berwick-upon-Tweed into a hub of creative energy, showing independent films and media art pieces.

- **Address**: Various places in Berwick-upon-Tweed, TD15
- **Cost**: Varies by event
- **Personal Experience**: The Berwick Film & Media Arts Festival is a feast for the senses. The mix of film shows, art pieces, and collaborative events creates a lively and engaging atmosphere. It's a great chance to study modern media in an ancient setting.

- Haltwhistle Walking Festival: Celebrating the beautiful scenery of Northumberland with guided walks ranging from gentle strolls to tough hikes, this fair caters to all types of walkers.

- **Address**: Various places around Haltwhistle, NE49
- **Cost:** Varies by walk
- **Personal Experience:** Participating in the Haltwhistle Walking Festival was a great way to discover the natural beauty of Northumberland. The guided walks are well-organized and interesting, with knowledgeable guides sharing insights about the area's history, plants, and wildlife. It's a great way to meet with fellow walkers and nature lovers.

Local Legends and Folklore: *Tales from the Borders*

Northumberland's rich past is entwined with a wealth of local tales and folklore, giving a magical layer to its scenery and historical sites. These stories passed down through generations, provide an interesting glimpse into the region's cultural history.

Highlights:

- The Laidly Worm of Spindleston Heugh: A famous Northumbrian tale about a princess turned into a dragon by her wicked stepmother. The story is linked with Bamburgh Castle and the nearby Spindlestone Heugh.

- **Location**: Bamburgh Castle, Bamburgh NE69 7DF
- **Personal Experience:** Hearing the tale of the Laidly Worm while visiting Bamburgh Castle added a magical layer to the experience. The tale brings the castle's old stones to life, filling the site with a feeling of magic and mystery.

- **The Chillingham Wild Cattle:** Chillingham Castle is home to a group of wild white cattle, said to be the remains of an ancient breed. The house itself is considered to be one of the most evil in Britain.

  - **Address**: Chillingham Castle, Alnwick NE66 5NJ
  - **Cost**: Adults £10.50, Children £6.50
  - **Personal Experience:** Visiting Chillingham Castle and seeing the wild animals was a unique adventure. The eerie atmosphere of the castle, mixed with the ghost stories told by the guides, made an exciting journey. It's a place where history and folklore combine in a strangely beautiful setting.

- **The Border Reivers:** Tales of the fearsome Border Reivers, raiders who stole across the Anglo-Scottish borders from the 13th to the 17th centuries, are sewn into the fabric of Northumberland's past.

- **Location**: Various places along the Anglo-Scottish border
- **Personal Experience:** Exploring the borders and hearing stories of the Reivers gave a sense of the anarchy and unrest of the past. Visiting the places connected with these tales, such as Hermitage Castle, offered a physical relationship to the region's chaotic past.

Northumberland's unique experiences offer a rich mix of stargazing, cultural events, and fascinating tales. Whether you're looking at the stars in Kielder's Dark Sky Park, immersing yourself in the lively local events, or diving into the region's history, each experience provides a unique and memorable way to connect with the heart and soul of Northumberland. Embrace these adventures and let them improve your trip through this charming area.

CHAPTER 7

Wildlife and Natural Wonders

Northumberland is a paradise for nature fans, boasting a wide range of wildlife and stunning natural landscapes. From the busy seabird colonies of the Farne Islands to the quiet woods and rivers hidden throughout the county, these natural wonders offer a fascinating experience for all who journey into the wilds of Northumberland.

Farne Islands: *A Seabird Spectacle*

The Farne Islands, located off the coast of Northumberland, are a home for wildlife, especially seabirds. These islands provide one of the most stunning wildlife adventures in the UK, especially during the breeding season.

Highlights:

- **Puffins:** Thousands of puffins nest on the islands from April to July, giving a lovely sight as they swoop and dive for fish.

- **Grey Seals**: The Farne Islands are home to a large number of grey seals. Seal pups can often be seen in the autumn months.
- **Diverse Birdlife**: Besides puffins, the islands host razorbills, guillemots, Arctic terns, and many other bird species.

Visitor Information:
- **Address**: Farne Islands, near Seahouses, Northumberland NE68 7SR
- **Cost:** Boat trips: Adults £20-£40, Children £12-£20 (prices vary by tour company and trip length)
- Personal Experience: Taking a boat trip to the Farne Islands was an amazing experience. The sight of thousands of puffins with their colored beaks, the chaos of bird calls, and the playful seals basking on the rocks made a lively and engaging experience with nature. The expert guides gave

interesting views into the lives of the island's people.

Red Squirrels and Wild Goats: *Wildlife Watching*

Northumberland's various settings are home to a range of wildlife, including the rare red squirrel and the hardy wild goats. Several sites within the county provide great chances for wildlife watching.

Highlights:
- **Red Squirrels**: One of the few places in England where red squirrels can still be found, Northumberland's woods offer a refuge for these charming creatures.
- **Wild Goats**: The Cheviot Hills are home to wild goats, descendants of old herds that have roamed the area for centuries.

Visitor Information:

- **Red Squirrels:** Best viewed in Kielder Forest and other wooded areas.

- **Address**: Kielder Forest, Northumberland NE48 1ER
- **Cost**: Free

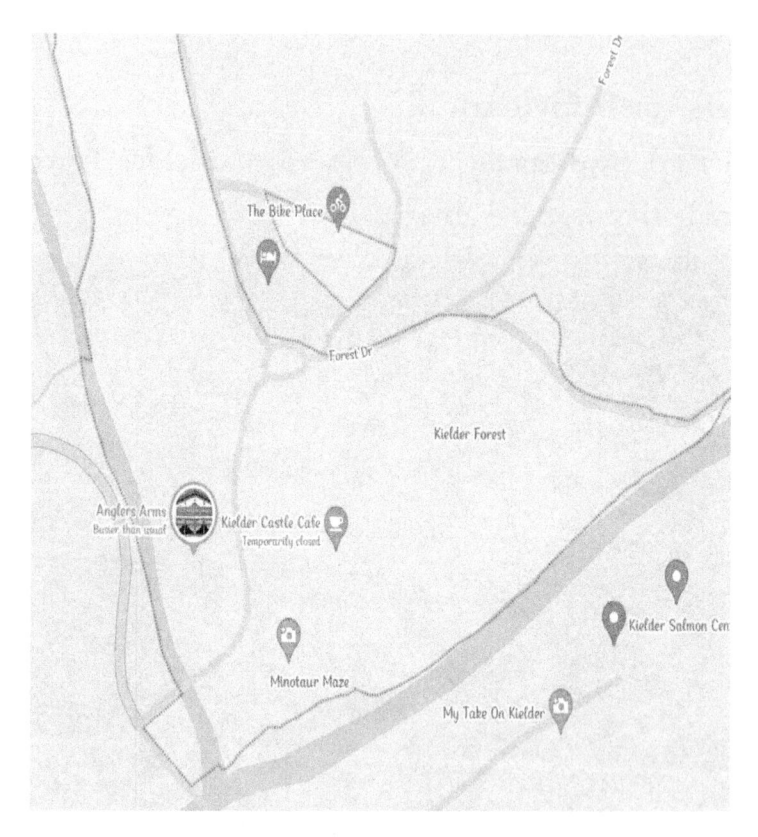

- **Personal Experience**: Spotting a red squirrel in Kielder Forest was a lovely highlight of my visit. These shy and quick creatures are a joy to watch as they dart among the trees. Early morning or late afternoon visits raise the chances of views.

- **Wild Goats**: Best viewed in the Cheviot Hills.

- **Address**: Cheviot Hills, near Wooler, Northumberland NE71
- **Cost**: Free
- **Personal Experience:** Encountering the wild goats of the Cheviots was an unplanned thrill. Their rough, majestic presence amidst the dramatic landscapes added a wild and ancient feel to the walk. It's a reminder of the wild spirit of Northumberland's countryside.

Waterfalls and Woodlands: *Hidden Natural Gems*

Northumberland is dotted with secret nature gems, from calm woods to charming rivers. These isolated spots offer peaceful escapes and are great for nature walks and quiet thoughts.

Highlights:
- **Hareshaw Linn**: A stunning waterfall near Bellingham, backed by old forest and rich in wildlife. The walk to the waterfall is through a magical setting of ferns and moss-covered trees.
- **Address**: Bellingham, Hexham NE48 2JP
- **Cost**: Free
- **Personal Experience**: The walk to Hareshaw Linn is a quiet and beautiful trip. The sound of the waterfall getting louder as you approach is thrilling. The lush grass and

the sight of the flowing water make it a great spot for photos and leisure.

- **Linhope Spout:** A beautiful 18-meter waterfall found in the Ingram Valley. The hike to Linhope Spout offers beautiful views of the nearby countryside.
    - **Address**: Ingram Valley, Alnwick NE66 4LT
    - **Cost**: Free
    - **Personal Experience:** Linhope Spout is a secret gem in the heart of Northumberland. The walk is relatively easy and the prize at the end, a strong waterfall falling into a deep

plunge pool, is well worth the effort. It's a great spot for a picnic or a cooling dip in the summer.

- **Thrunton Wood**: A beautiful woodland area with a network of walking and riding trails, giving panoramic views over the nearby landscapes.

- **Address**: Thrunton, Alnwick NE66 4SD
- **Cost**: Free
- **Personal Experience**: Thrunton Wood offers a peaceful getaway into nature. The tracks are well-marked and vary in difficulty, making them available for all types of walkers. The views from the top of Thrunton Crag are beautiful, offering a wide picture of the countryside.

Northumberland's wildlife and natural wonders are a testament to the region's rich variety and unspoiled beauty. From the busy seabird colonies of the Farne Islands to the calm forests and secret waterfalls, these natural sites offer a serene and captivating break. Embrace the chance to connect with nature, find secret gems, and make lasting memories in the wild heart of Northumberland.

CHAPTER 8

Where Couples Can Visit

Northumberland is a charming location for lovers wanting romance and excitement. From private beach walks and luxury retreats to personal eating experiences, this chapter will guide you through the most romantic spots for an amazing trip.

Romantic Beach Walks: *Embleton Bay and Beyond*

Northumberland's shore offers some of the most beautiful and quiet beaches in the UK, perfect for a romantic walk with your loved one. Embleton Bay, with its wide sands and amazing views, is a standout location for lovers.

Highlights:

- **Embleton Bay:** This beautiful bay offers vast sandy beaches with views of the famous Dunstanburgh Castle ruins in the distance. It's an ideal spot for a relaxed walk, especially at sunset.

- **Address**: Embleton, Alnwick NE66 3XQ
- **Cost**: Free
- **Personal Experience:** Walking along Embleton Bay with the sound of waves lapping at our feet and the outline of Dunstanburgh Castle against the setting sun was simply beautiful. The quiet surroundings

and the natural beauty of the bay create a private and peaceful atmosphere.

- Bamburgh Beach: With its wide, golden sands and the grand Bamburgh Castle as a setting, this beach is great for a romantic walk and a picnic.

- **Address**: Bamburgh, NE69 7DF
- **Cost**: Free
- **Personal Experience**: Bamburgh Beach is a place where history and nature meet beautifully. Strolling hand-in-hand with

Bamburgh Castle looming above us felt like a scene from a fairy tale. It's a great spot for lovers who respect both historical mystery and natural beauty.

Luxurious Getaways: *Spa Hotels and Boutique B&Bs*

For couples wanting a luxurious getaway, Northumberland offers a variety of spa hotels and small bed and breakfasts that provide the right mix of warmth, care, and luxury.

Highlights:
- **Doxford Hall Hotel & gym**: This elegant country house hotel offers luxurious rooms, a full-service gym, and fine dining. It's an ideal spot for lovers looking to relax and refresh in a quiet setting.

- **Address**: Doxford Hall, Chathill NE67 5DN

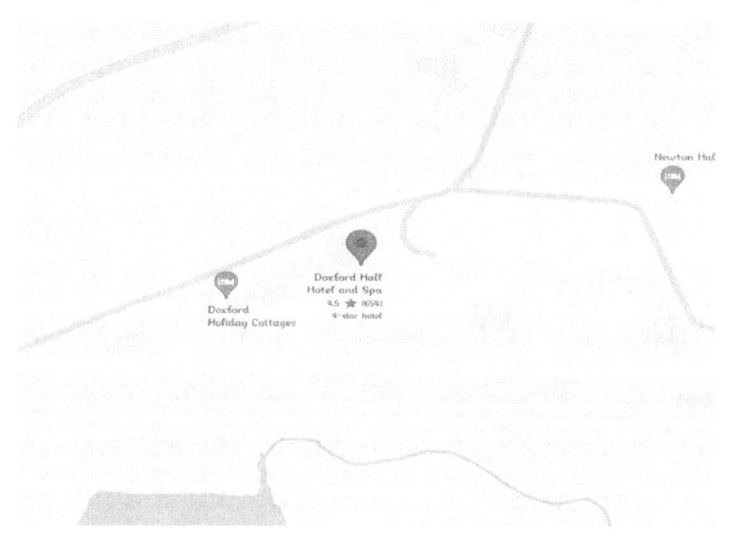

- **Cost**: Rooms from £150 per night; spa services vary
- **Personal Experience:** Our stay at Doxford Hall was a wonderful getaway. The spa facilities were top-notch, and the quiet grounds of the farm provided a tranquil setting for a romantic weekend. The evening meal in the fine dining restaurant was excellent, adding a touch of class to our stay.

- **The Cookie Jar:** Located in the heart of Alnwick, this boutique hotel offers charming rooms with a unique mix of modern comfort and historic character. It's great for lovers looking for a cozy and private setting.

- **Address**: 12 Bailiffgate, Alnwick NE66 1LU
- **Cost:** Rooms from £120 per night
- **Personal Experience:** Staying at The Cookie Jar was like a home away from home. The individual service and cozy setting made it a great escape. We enjoyed exploring

Alnwick during the day and escaping to our nicely equipped room in the evening.

- Eshott Hall: This Georgian country house hotel is set on beautiful grounds and offers elegant rooms and fine meals. It's an ideal spot for a romantic getaway in the countryside.

- **Address**: Eshott, Morpeth NE65 9EN
- **Cost**: Rooms from £140 per night
- **Personal Experience:** Eshott Hall is the ideal of beauty. The grand house, the beautifully planted grounds, and the luxury

rooms provided an ideal setting for our holiday. Dining in the big hall by candlelight was a highlight of our stay.

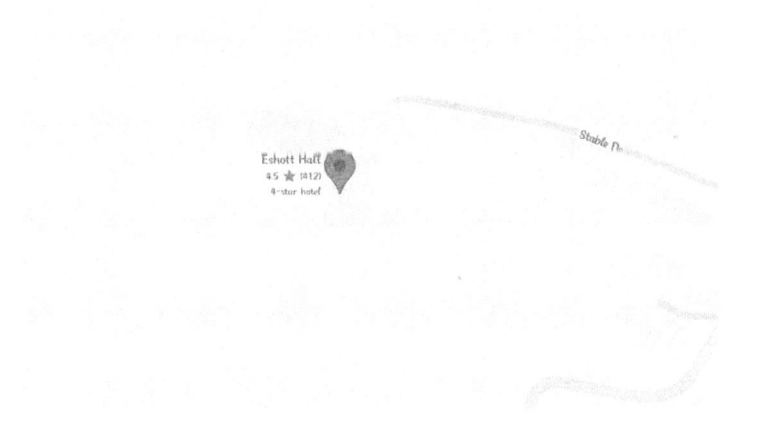

Candlelit Dinners: *Top Romantic Restaurants*

Northumberland boasts a range of places great for a lovely evening out. From fine eating establishments to cozy bistros, these places offer private settings and excellent food.

Highlights:

- The Potted Lobster: Located in Bamburgh, this charming restaurant is known for its fresh fish and cozy surroundings. Perfect for a romantic dinner, it offers a private setting and delicious meals.

- **Address**: 3 Lucker Rd, Bamburgh NE69 7BS
- **Cost**: Mains from £15-£25
- **Personal Experience:** Dining at The Potted Lobster was a private and pleasant event. The fish was fresh and perfectly cooked, and the warm, welcoming setting made it feel like a special occasion. The careful service and delicious desserts made the evening memorable.

- The Old Boathouse: Situated in Amble, this seaside restaurant offers beautiful views and a

---

89| Northumberland Travel Guide 2024

menu that features locally sourced products. It's an ideal spot for a lovely meal with a view.

- **Address**: Leazes St, Amble NE65 0AA

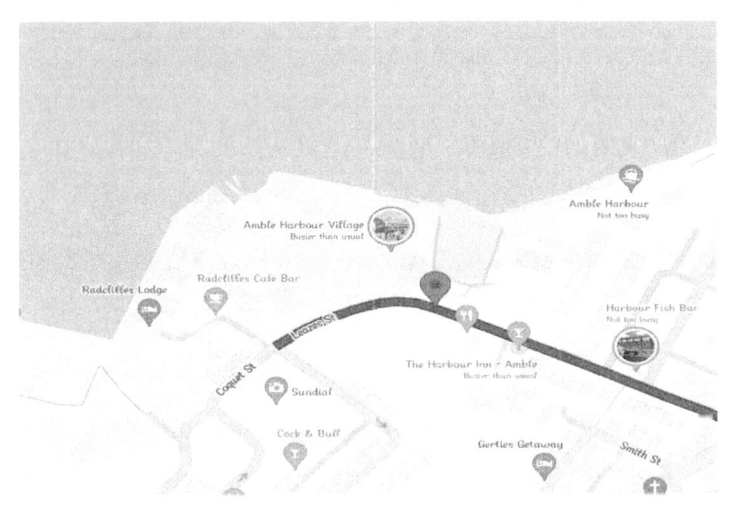

- **Cost**: Mains from £14-£28
- **Personal Experience:** The Old Boathouse provided a great love setting with its waterside site and wonderful fish. Watching the sunset over the bay while having our food was truly special. The relaxed yet elegant setting made for a wonderful evening.

- **Jaspers cafe:** Located in Amble, this cozy cafe offers a warm, personal eating experience with a menu that celebrates local food. It's great for a quiet, romantic dinner.

- **Address**: 57-59 Queen St, Amble NE65 0DA
- **Cost:** Mains from £12-£22
- **Personal Experience:** Jaspers Bistro had a friendly and private vibe that was great for a lovely dinner. The menu featured a wonderful selection of local foods, and the candlelit setting added a bit of romance. It was a lovely event that we both valued.

Northumberland offers a wealth of love experiences for couples, from enchanting beach walks and luxury getaways to private light dinners. Whether you're enjoying a special event or simply looking to spend quality time together, these places provide the perfect setting for love and romance. Embrace these times and let Northumberland's beauty create memorable memories for you and your partner.

CHAPTER 9:

Where Kids Can Visit

Northumberland is not only a playground for adults but also a wonderland for children, offering a variety of sights and activities to spark their imagination and sense of adventure. From magical gardens to exciting animal encounters, this chapter will guide you through the top places where kids can let their minds soar and create lasting memories.

Alnwick Garden: *A Wonderland for All Ages*

Alnwick Garden is a beautiful haven that facinates tourists of all ages with its charming features and interactive experiences. From charming gardens to exciting play areas, there's something for every member of the family to enjoy.

Highlights:

- The Poison Garden: Discover a collection of dangerous plants from around the world in this interesting park, where children can learn about the dangers of certain botanical species under the watchful eye of experienced guides.

- The Treehouse: Let ideas run wild in the biggest wooden treehouse in the world, complete with rope bridges, treetop paths, and secret hideaways. It's a wonderful place where children can play and discover to their hearts' joy.

- The Grand Cascade: Marvel at the amazing water feature, featuring a series of falling waterfalls and streams that flow down to a reflecting pool. Children can enjoy watching the synced water shows and even make a wish at the base of the waterfall.

Visitor Information:

- **Address**: Alnwick Garden, Denwick Lane, Alnwick NE66 1YU

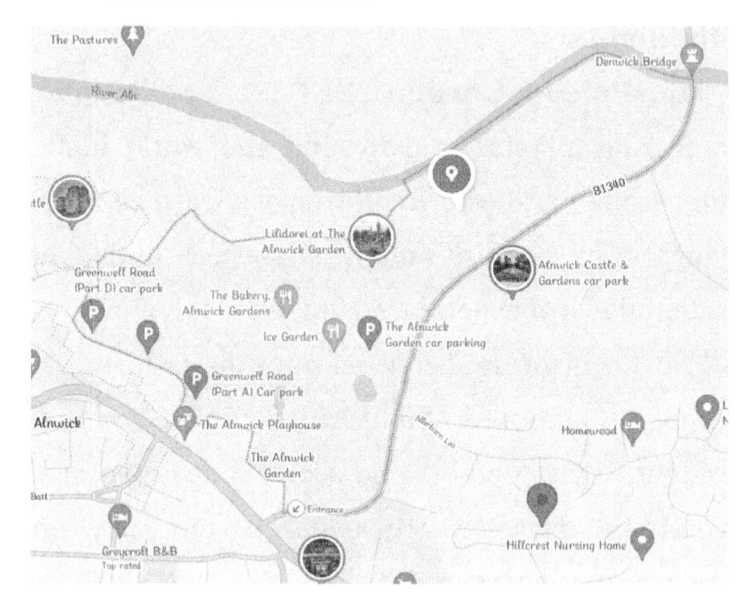

- **Cost:** Adults £12.10, Children £5.45, Family £29.00

- Personal Experience: Exploring Alnwick Garden with my children was like going into a fairytale world. The Poison Garden was both educational and interesting, while the Treehouse sparked their fantasies with its magical atmosphere. The Grand Cascade offered a beautiful setting for family pictures and times of wonder.

Northumberland Zoo: *A Family Adventure*

Northumberland Zoo offers an exciting chance for children to get up close and personal with a range of foreign and local animals. With educational exhibits, daily talks, and hands-on experiences, it's a family-friendly location that blends education with fun.

Highlights:
- **Animal Encounters:** From lemurs and meerkats to wallabies and capybaras, children can meet a wide range of animals from around the world. Interactive feeding sessions and keeper talks

provide interesting insights into their habits and surroundings.

- **Play Areas:** The zoo features adventure playgrounds and picnic areas where children can burn off energy and enjoy outdoor fun. From climbing frames to zip lines, there's no lack of things to keep little ones amused.

- **Educational Programs:** The zoo offers educational classes and experiences meant to spark interest and conservation knowledge in young guests. From animal-touching lessons to behind-the-scenes walks, children can learn about the value of wildlife protection in a fun and interesting way.

Visitor Information:

- **Address**: Northumberland Zoo, Eshottheugh Farm, Felton, Morpeth NE65 9QH
- **Cost**: Adults £9.95, Children £7.95, Family £34.95

- **Personal Experience:** Visiting Northumberland Zoo was an exciting adventure for my children. They were intrigued by the wide range of animals and liked learning about their habits and environments from the knowledgeable staff. The engaging displays and play areas provided a perfect mix of education and fun for the whole family.

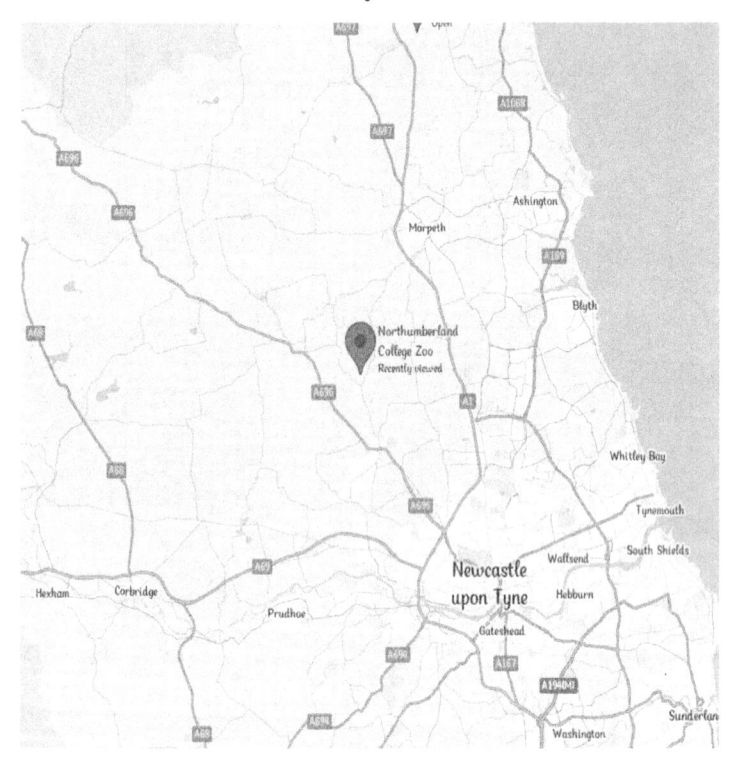

Bamburgh Beach: *Fun and Frolic by the Sea*

Bamburgh Beach is a haven for children, giving miles of golden sands, rolling waves, and endless chances for outdoor fun. Whether making sandcastles, playing in the sea, or discovering rock pools, children can unleash their creativity and imagination in this seaside paradise.

Highlights:

- **Sandcastle Building**: With its vast stretch of soft sand, Bamburgh Beach is the perfect stage for budding builders to build tall sandcastles and complex sculptures. Let their thoughts run wild as they make their beach wonders.

- **Rock Pooling:** Tour the interesting world of rock pools, filled with marine life waiting to be found. From crabs and starfish to sea anemones and tiny fish, children can learn about seaside ecosystems while having fun.

- Beach Games: From beach volleyball and frisbee to kite flying and beach cricket, there's no lack of games and activities to keep children entertained on Bamburgh Beach. Let them run, jump, and play to their heart's content in this natural playground by the sea.

Visitor Information:
- **Address:** Bamburgh Beach, Bamburgh, NE69 7DF
- **Cost**: Free
- **Personal Experience:** Spending a day at Bamburgh Beach with my children was a happy experience. They loved playing in the waves, collecting shells, and making sandcastles along the beach. Exploring the rock pools showed a secret world of interesting animals, sparking their curiosity and sense of wonder.

Northumberland offers a wealth of sites and activities where kids can release their ideas, learn about the natural world, and create long moments with their families. Whether discovering beautiful gardens, meeting exotic animals, or playing on sandy beaches, children will find endless opportunities for adventure and discovery in this enchanting corner of England.

CHAPTER 10

Travel Tips and Practical Information

To ensure your trip through Northumberland is easy and enjoyable, this part offers important travel tips and useful information. From exploring the region to finding the right place to stay and enjoying local foods, here's everything you need to know to make the most of your visit.

Getting Around: *Transport Tips*

Navigating Northumberland's various environments takes some planning. Whether you're exploring busy cities or remote areas, here are the best ways to get around.

Public Transport:

- Buses: Arriva North East and Go North East run large bus lines serving most towns and villages. The X18 seaside Clipper, for example, offers beautiful seaside paths.

- **Cost:** Day tickets from £5.50 for adults and £4 for children; North East tour ticket costs £10.50 per day for unlimited travel.
- **Tip:** Purchase a North East tour ticket for unlimited travel across different bus routes.
- **Personal Experience**: Taking the X18 Coastal Clipper was an event in itself. The scenic views along the coast were beautiful, and the ease of hopping on and off allowed us to tour charming towns at our own pace.

- Trains: Northern Train and LNER provide train services connecting major places like Newcastle, Alnwick, and Berwick-upon-Tweed.

- **Cost**: Advance fares from Newcastle to Berwick-upon-Tweed start at £10; children's tickets are half price.
- **Tip**: Book tickets in advance for cheaper fares and check routes for less frequent country services.
- **Personal Experience:** Traveling by train offers a comfortable and beautiful way to see the scenery. The trip from Newcastle to Alnwick was particularly beautiful, with rising hills and historical sites visible from the window.

Car Hire:

- **Renting a Car:** For freedom, consider renting a car from Newcastle International Airport or city centers. Major car rental companies like Avis, Hertz, and Enterprise are offered.
  - **Cost**: Daily rates start from £30, based on the car type and hire length.

- **Tip:** Ensure you have an accurate GPS or map as cell service can be spotty in remote places.
- **Personal Experience:** Hiring a car gave us the freedom to discover off-the-beaten-path places. Driving through the Cheviot Hills and along the coast was a memorable experience, giving beautiful views and the freedom to stop wherever we wanted.

- **Driving Tips:** Northumberland's roads range from motorways to small country streets. Drive carefully and be aware of wildlife crossing country roads.
  - **Tip**: Fill up on fuel before going into remote places as gas shops can be sparse.
  - **Personal Experience**: Navigating the country roads of Northumberland was both exciting and a bit difficult. The small roads needed careful driving, but the stunning scenery made it all worthwhile.

Riding:

- Bike Rentals: Northumberland is ideal for riding fans. Rent bikes from nearby shops like Chain Reaction Cycles in Newcastle or Pedal-Power in Hexham.

- **Cost:** Daily bike hire from £15-£25.
- **Tip**: Tour Sustrans National Cycle Network paths, particularly Route 1 which runs along the beautiful shoreline.
- **Personal Experience:** Cycling through Northumberland offered a unique view of its natural beauty. The coastal route offered spectacular sea views, while inland trails took us through lovely villages and lush countryside.

Where to Stay: *From Luxury to Cozy B&Bs*

Northumberland offers a range of places to meet all tastes and budgets. Whether you prefer luxurious hotels or lovely bed and breakfasts, you'll find the right place to rest your head.

Luxury Stays:

- Doxford Hall Hotel & Spa: A beautiful country house hotel offering luxury rooms, a full-service spa, and fine dining.

- **Address**: Doxford Hall, Chathill NE67 5DN
- **Cost:** Rooms from £150 per night
- **Highlight**: The quiet spa facilities and beautifully planted grounds provide a perfect escape.
- **Personal Experience:** Our stay at Doxford Hall was a luxury getaway. The spa treatments were wonderful, and walking through the groomed grounds was incredibly relaxing. The room was sumptuous, and the service was excellent.

- **Matfen Hall**: A grand estate with lavish rooms, a golf course, and a spa, set amidst beautiful countryside.

- **Address**: Matfen, Newcastle upon Tyne NE20 0RH
- **Cost**: Rooms from £160 per night
- **Highlight**: The blend of historical charm and modern luxury, along with excellent leisure facilities.
- **Personal Experience:** Matfen Hall felt like a step back in time with its grand building and green fields. We loved the spa and had a lovely dinner at the on-site restaurant, making it a memorable stay.

Mid-Range Hotels:

- **The Cookie Jar:** A boutique hotel in Alnwick giving cozy, stylish rooms and a warm atmosphere.

- **Address**: 12 Bailiffgate, Alnwick NE66 1LU
- **Cost**: Rooms from £120 per night

- **Highlight**: Proximity to Alnwick Castle and Garden, great for exploring the town.
- **Personal Experience**: The Cookie Jar had a friendly and homey feel. The staff were incredibly friendly, and the breakfast was a highlight of our stay. The central position made it easy to tour Alnwick.

- **The Amble Inn**: A welcoming inn with comfortable rooms and a filling breakfast, located in the coastal town of Amble.
  - **Address:** Sandpiper Way, Amble NE65 0FF
  - **Cost**: Rooms from £90 per night
  - **Highlight**: Easy entry to the harbor and nearby sites like Warkworth Castle.
  - **Personal Experience:** Staying at The Amble Inn was great for our coastal adventures. The rooms were clean and cozy, and the filling meals powered our days of travel.

Cozy B&Bs:

- Market Cross Guest House: A lovely B&B in Belford giving individually decorated rooms and a homemade breakfast.

- **Address:** 1 Church St, Belford NE70 7LS
- **Cost**: Rooms from £85 per night
- **Highlight:** Friendly hosts and a lovely garden setting.
- **Personal Experience:** Market Cross Guest House felt like a home away from home. The hosts were incredibly friendly, and the cooked food was a treat. The park was a peaceful place to relax after a day of travel.

- Redfoot Lea: A converted farm steading giving cozy rooms and a delicious breakfast near Alnwick.

- **Address**: Greensfield Moor Farm, Alnwick NE66 2HH
- **Cost:** Rooms from £95 per night
- **Highlight**: The peaceful country setting and closeness to Alnwick's sights.

111| Northumberland Travel Guide 2024

- **Personal Experience:** Redfoot Lea offered a lovely and calm stay. The rooms were nicely furnished, and the food was excellent. It was a perfect base for visiting Alnwick and the local scenery.

Local Cuisine: *Must-Try Northumbrian Dishes*

Sampling Northumberland's local food is a must. From hearty comfort food to gourmet delights, here are some meals and places you shouldn't miss.

Must-Try Dishes:
- **Stottie Cake:** A thick, round bread typically served with bacon or pease pudding. Perfect for breakfast or a snack.

- **Northumberland Lamb:** Locally grown lamb, often featured in roasts or soups, known for its soft and tasty meat.
- **Craster Kippers:** Smoked herring from the village of Craster, known for their unique and delicious smoky taste.

Top Dining Spots:

- The Treehouse Restaurant at Alnwick Garden: Dine among the treetops in this unique setting, offering fresh and locally sourced meals.

- **Address:** Alnwick Garden, Denwick Lane, Alnwick NE66 1YU
- **Cost:** Mains from £15-£30
- **Highlight:** The magical setting and creative food.
- **Personal Experience:** Dining at The Treehouse Restaurant was an amazing event. The mood was charming, and the food was superb. It was a great place for a special

meal, surrounded by the natural beauty of the garden.

- The Potted Lobster: Located in Bamburgh, this restaurant is famous for its seafood, especially fresh lobster and crab.

- **Address**: 3 Lucker Rd, Bamburgh NE69 7BS
- **Cost**: Mains from £15-£25
- **Highlight**: The cozy setting and the fine seafood meals.
- **Personal Experience:** The Potted Lobster was a wonderful dining treat. The fish was incredibly fresh, and the lobster was cooked to perfection. The warm, welcoming setting made it a pleasant eating experience.

- The Jolly Fisherman: A seaside bar in Craster offering classic meals and beautiful sea views.

- **Address**: Haven Hill, Craster NE66 3TR
- **Cost**: Mains from £12-£22

- **Highlight**: The best spot to try Craster kippers and enjoy the beautiful seashore.
- **Personal Experience:** Enjoying a meal at The Jolly Fisherman was a highlight of our trip. The views of the sea were amazing, and the Craster kippers were wonderful. The relaxed, friendly vibe of the bar made it a great spot to unwind after a day of traveling.

With these useful tips and travel ideas, your journey through Northumberland will be smooth and fun. Whether you're traveling the beautiful roads, finding the right place to stay, or indulging in local tastes.

CHAPTER 11

Day Trips and Itineraries

Northumberland is brimming with attractions and experiences, making it perfect for both short and extended visits. To help you make the most of your time, here are some carefully curated itineraries for different types of travelers. Whether you're visiting for a weekend, with your family, or on a romantic escape, these itineraries will ensure you see the best of Northumberland.

Perfect Weekend in Northumberland

Day 1: Exploring Historic Alnwick
➢ **Morning**:
- **Alnwick Castle**: Start your day with a visit to the iconic Alnwick Castle, famous for its rich history and as a filming location for Harry Potter.

- **Address**: Alnwick Castle, Alnwick NE66 1NQ
- **Cost**: Adults £16.50, Children £8.50
- **Personal Experience:** Walking through the grand halls and lush gardens of Alnwick Castle felt like stepping into a fairy tale. The kids loved the dragon quest activities, and we all enjoyed the breathtaking views from the battlements.

- **Alnwick Garden**: Just a short walk away, tour the stunning Alnwick Garden with its impressive Grand Cascade and magical Treehouse Restaurant.
  - **Cost**: Adults £12.10, Children £5.45
  - **Personal Experience:** The garden's innovative design and interactive features, like the Poison Garden, made for a delightful and educational experience. Lunch in the Treehouse Restaurant was a unique treat.

➢ **Afternoon:**

- **Barter Books:** Spend some time in one of the largest second-hand bookstores in Europe, located in a converted Victorian railway station.
  - **Address**: Alnwick Station, Alnwick NE66 2NP
  - **Cost:** Free entry (costs vary for books)
  - **Personal Experience**: The cozy atmosphere and vast collection of books made Barter Books a perfect place to relax and find hidden literary treasures.

Day 2: Coastal Charms and Castles
➢ **Morning**:
- **Bamburgh Castle**: Head to the coast to visit Bamburgh Castle, a majestic fortress with stunning sea views.
  - **Address**: Bamburgh, NE69 7DF
  - **Cost**: Adults £12.50, Children £6.15
  - **Personal Experience**: Exploring the castle's rooms and ramparts while hearing the waves crash below was unforgettable.

The museum exhibits were fascinating, particularly the Armstrong and Aviation Artifacts.

➢ **Afternoon**:

- Holy Island of Lindisfarne: Drive to the Holy Island of Lindisfarne, accessible via a tidal causeway. Tour the historic priory and enjoy the serene landscapes.

- **Address**: Holy Island, Berwick-upon-Tweed TD15 2RX
- **Cost:** Adults £9.60, Children £5.80
- **Personal Experience:** The island's mystical atmosphere and historical significance made it a highlight of our trip. Watching the tide come in and cover the causeway was a unique experience.

Family-Friendly Adventure

Day 1: Fun and Learning in Alnwick

➢ **Morning**:

- **Alnwick Garden**: Start your family adventure at the Alnwick Garden with its interactive and child-friendly features.

- **Cost**: Adults £12.10, Children £5.45
- **Personal Experience:** The kids were mesmerized by the Grand Cascade and had a blast in the labyrinth and adventure playground.

➢ **Afternoon:**

- **Northumberland Zoo:** A short drive away, Northumberland Zoo offers a chance for kids to see and learn about various animals.

- **Address**: Eshottheugh Farm, Felton, Morpeth NE65 9QH
- **Cost**: Adults £9.95, Children £7.95

- **Personal Experience:** The zoo was a hit with the kids, who loved feeding the lemurs and watching the meerkats. The staff were friendly and knowledgeable, adding to the educational experience.

Day 2: Beaches and Castles

➢ **Morning**:

- **Bamburgh Beach:** Spend a morning on Bamburgh Beach, where kids can build sandcastles and tour rock pools.
  - **Cost**: Free
  - **Personal Experience**: The kids loved running along the beach and collecting shells. The backdrop of Bamburgh Castle made it feel like a scene from a storybook.

➢ **Afternoon**:

- **Bamburgh Castle:** After the beach, visit the nearby Bamburgh Castle for a family-friendly historical adventure.

- **Cost**: Adults £12.50, Children £6.15
- **Personal Experience**: The castle's interactive exhibits and stunning views kept the kids entertained and engaged. The story of the castle's history fascinated us all.

Romantic Escapes and Hidden Getaways

Day 1: Coastal Romance
➢ **Morning**:
- **Embleton Bay:** Start your romantic getaway with a walk along the secluded and picturesque Embleton Bay.
- **Cost:** Free
- **Personal Experience:** Walking hand-in-hand along the pristine sands with Dunstanburgh Castle in the distance was incredibly romantic. The tranquility and

natural beauty made it a perfect spot for a quiet moment together.

➢ **Afternoon:**
- **Dunstanburgh Castle**: Tour the ruins of Dunstanburgh Castle, accessible by a scenic coastal walk.
- **Address:** Craster, Alnwick NE66 3TT
- **Cost:** Adults £6.90, Children £4.10
- **Personal Experience:** The walk to the castle offered stunning views, and exploring the ruins was a unique experience. The solitude of the location added to its romantic charm.

Day 2: Luxury and Relaxation
➢ Morning:
- **Doxford Hall Hotel & Spa**: Indulge in a spa morning at Doxford Hall Hotel & Spa, enjoying treatments and relaxation together.
- **Address**: Doxford Hall, Chathill NE67 5DN
- **Cost**: Spa packages from £45 per person

- **Personal Experience:** The serene setting and luxurious treatments made for a perfect start to our day. Relaxing in the spa facilities together was a wonderful way to unwind and reconnect.

➤ **Afternoon**:

- **The Treehouse Restaurant:** End your day with a romantic dinner at The Treehouse Restaurant in Alnwick Garden.
  - **Cost:** Mains from £15-£30
  - **Personal Experience:** Dining among the treetops in this enchanting restaurant was a magical experience. The intimate setting and delicious food made it an unforgettable evening.

With these tailored itineraries, you can tour Northumberland's rich history, stunning landscapes, and charming towns in ways that best suit your interests and needs. Whether it's a weekend escape, a family adventure, or a romantic getaway, these plans ensure you experience the best of what this enchanting region has to offer.

CHAPTER 12

Beyond Northumberland

While Northumberland offers an abundance of sights and experiences, traveling beyond its limits reveals a patchwork of diverse scenery, rich history, and cultural treasures. This part invites you to visit nearby regions, from the charming Scottish Borders to the historic towns of Durham and York, and beyond, ensuring your English trip is both enriching and memorable.

Excursions to the Scottish Borders

Berwick-upon-Tweed: A Border Town with History

- **Overview**: Nestled on the banks of the River Tweed, Berwick-upon-Tweed is a quintessential border town soaked in centuries of history and filled with architectural charm.

- Highlights:

- Berwick Walls: Embark on a stroll along the well-preserved Elizabethan walls encircling the town, offering panoramic views of the rough shore and rolling farmland.

- Berwick Barracks: Step back in time at this imposing military complex, now home to a fascinating museum and halls that chronicle the town's turbulent past.

- **Address**: Berwick-upon-Tweed TD15 1DF
- **Cost**: Free to tour the town; entry to Berwick Barracks is £5.60 for adults, £3.40 for children.
- **Personal Experience:** The formidable bastions of Berwick Walls allowed us sweeping views of the nearby landscape while diving into the barracks' exhibits submerged us in Berwick's storied military history.

Kelso and Floors Castle: *A Scottish Delight*

- **Overview:** Venture across the border into Kelso, a picturesque town set amidst green farmland, and discover the magnificent Floors Castle, a testament to Scotland's architectural grandeur.

- **Highlights:**

- **Floors Castle:** Embark on a regal journey through Scotland's biggest living castle, where rich interiors, resplendent grounds, and captivating art collections await.

- **Address**: Kelso, Roxburghshire TD5 7SF
- **Cost:** Admission to castle and gardens: £16.50 for adults, £8.50 for children.
- **Personal Experience:** Exploring the lavish rooms of Floors Castle, adorned with priceless carpets and paintings, took us to an era of royal glory amid beautifully planted gardens.

Melrose and Abbotsford: *Literary and Historical Riches*

- **Overview:** Dig into the literary legacy and medieval marvels of Melrose, a quaint town famous for its ancient abbey ruins, before starting on a journey to Abbotsford, the family home of Sir Walter Scott.

 - Highlights:

- **Melrose Abbey:** Wander amidst the haunting ruins of Melrose Abbey, an architectural wonder going back to the 12th century, and marvel at its finely cut stone details.

- **Address**: Melrose TD6 9LG
- **Cost**: Admission: £6.00 for adults, £3.60 for children.
- **- Abbotsford House:** Immerse yourself in the world of Scotland's beloved literary figure, Sir Walter Scott, as you discover the

rich interiors and beautiful grounds of Abbotsford House.

- **Address**: Abbotsford, Melrose TD6 9BQ
- **Cost**: Admission to house and gardens: £12.00 for adults, £6.00 for children.
- **Personal Experience:** Our journey through Melrose Abbey's time-worn arches evoked a sense of respect for Scotland's ancient heritage, while Abbotsford House offered a fascinating glimpse into the life and literary works of Sir Walter Scott amidst bucolic surroundings.

Exploring Nearby Durham and Yorkshire

Durham: *A City of Cathedral and Castle*

- **Overview:** Embark on a journey to Durham, where the UNESCO World Heritage Site of Durham Cathedral and Castle stands as a testament to the city's ongoing spiritual and physical importance.

- Highlights:

- **Durham Cathedral**: Marvel at the awe-inspiring beauty of Durham Cathedral, a masterpiece of Norman architecture famous for its high domes, detailed stone carvings, and serene cloisters.

- **Address**: Durham DH1 3EH
- **Cost**: Free entry (donations accepted).

- **Durham Castle**: Dig into the past of Durham Castle, a Norman fortress turned into a famous university college, and embark on guided tours to uncover its secrets.

- **Address**: Palace Green, Durham DH1 3RW
- **Cost**: Guided tour: £5.00 for adults, £4.00 for children.
- **Personal Experience**: Our ascent to the heights of Durham Cathedral's tower repaid us with breathtaking panoramas of the city's

medieval skyline, while the castle's hidden rooms unveiled tales of bygone wars and educational pursuits.

York: Medieval Marvels and Modern Delights

- Overview: Journey south to York, a city where ancient walls embrace a treasure trove of medieval streetscapes, cultural landmarks, and modern delights.

- Highlights:

- York Minster: Stand in awe before the celestial glory of York Minster, one of Europe's biggest Gothic churches, adorned with magnificent stained glass windows and elaborate stone carvings.

- **Address**: Deangate, York YO1 7HH
- **Cost:** Admission: £11.50 for adults, £4.50 for children.

- **The Shambles:** Lose yourself in the winding alleys of The Shambles, a medieval street lined with timber-framed buildings housing small shops, bars, and craft stores.

  - **Cost**: Free to tour.
  - **Personal Experience:** Ascending the vertiginous heights of York Minster's central tower gave us a bird's-eye view of the city's historic heart, while wandering through the timeworn lanes of The Shambles evoked pictures of a bygone age brought to life.

- **Whitby**: Coastal Charm and Gothic Splendor

- **Overview**: Embark on a coastal journey to Whitby, a beautiful harbor town steeped in maritime history and honored by Bram Stoker's famous tale, "Dracula."

  - Highlights:

- **Whitby Abbey:** Ascend the windswept rocks to Whitby Abbey, a frightening figure perched atop East Cliff, and lose yourself in its Gothic glory and macabre tales.

- **Address:** Abbey Lane, Whitby YO22 4JT
- **Cost:** *Admission:* £10.90 for adults, £6.50 for children.

- **Whitby Harbour:** Wander along the paved quaysides of Whitby Harbour, where fishing boats bob gently in the chilly embrace of the North Sea, and savor the best catch at harborside cafes.

- **Cost:** Free to tour.
- **Personal Experience:** Our climb to the windswept heights of Whitby Abbey took us to a world of Gothic romance and hidden secrets, while the busy quaysides of Whitby Harbour offered a taste of maritime magic amidst the salty tang of sea air.

Continuing Your English Adventure

Lake District: A Haven for Nature Lovers

- Overview: Embark on a journey of natural discovery in the Lake District, a wide area of rocky fells, shimmering lakes, and green valleys that have fascinated poets, artists, and nature lovers for centuries.

 - Highlights:

- Lake Windermere: Embark on a leisurely cruise across the tranquil waters of Lake Windermere, England's largest natural lake, and soak in the stunning panoramas of rolling hills and wooded shores.

- **Cost**: Boat trips start from £10.00 per person.

 - Scafell Pike: Ascend to the lofty heights of Scafell Pike, England's highest peak, and conquer its rough top for awe-inspiring views of the nearby peaks and valleys.

- **Personal Experience:** Our journey across the smooth surface of Lake Windermere revealed a world of peace and sublime beauty, while the exciting ascent of Scafell Pike tested our mettle and repaid us with views that stretched to the distance.

Hadrian's Wall: *A Roman Legacy*

- **Overview**: Embark on a trip through time along Hadrian's Wall, a famous Roman border that spans the breadth of northern England, and discover the secrets of its ancient defenses and villages.

 - **Highlights:**

- **Housesteads Roman Fort:** tour the atmospheric ruins of Housesteads Roman Fort, perched atop wild crags, and trace the footsteps of Roman legionnaires along the ancient walls.

- **Address**: Haydon Bridge, Hexham NE47 6NN
- **Cost**: Adults £9.60, Children £5.80.

 - Vindolanda: Dig into the rich weave of Roman life at Vindolanda, a historical site filled with objects and insights into the daily routines of soldiers and citizens.

- **Address:** Bardon Mill, Hexham NE47 7JN
- **Cost**: Adults £7.50, Children £4.50.
- **Personal Experience:** Our journey along Hadrian's Wall submerged us in the sounds of ancient societies, while the digs at Vindolanda offered a fascinating glimpse into the lives of those who once walked these famous lands.

North York Moors: Rugged Beauty and Quaint Villages - Overview: Embark on a journey of natural discovery amidst the wild landscapes of the North York Moors, where heather-clad moors, quiet dales, and beautiful villages await.

 - Highlights:

- Goathland: Journey to the idyllic village of Goathland, set amidst rolling hills and green fields, and immerse yourself in the timeless charm of its rustic houses and wandering paths.

- Personal Experience: Our stay in Goathland took us to a world of rural calm, where sheep grazed on green slopes and the sounds of village life echoed through the valley.

Lake District: *A Haven for Nature Lovers*

- Overview: Embark on a journey of natural discovery in the Lake District, a wide area of rocky fells, shimmering lakes, and green valleys that have fascinated poets, artists, and nature lovers for centuries.

- Highlights:

- **Lake Windermere**: Embark on a leisurely cruise across the tranquil waters of Lake Windermere, England's largest natural lake, and soak in the stunning panoramas of rolling hills and wooded shores.

- **Cost**: Boat trips start from £10.00 per person.
- **Scafell Pike**: Ascend to the lofty heights of Scafell Pike, England's highest peak, and conquer its rough top for awe-inspiring views of the nearby peaks and valleys.
- **Personal Experience**: Our journey across the smooth surface of Lake Windermere revealed a world of peace and sublime beauty, while the exciting ascent of Scafell

Pike tested our mettle and repaid us with views that stretched to the distance.

Hadrian's Wall: *A Roman Legacy*

- Overview: Embark on a trip through time along Hadrian's Wall, a famous Roman border that spans the breadth of northern England, and discover the secrets of its ancient defenses and villages.

 - Highlights:

- **Housesteads Roman Fort:** tour the atmospheric ruins of Housesteads Roman Fort, perched atop wild crags, and trace the footsteps of Roman legionnaires along the ancient walls.

- **Address**: Haydon Bridge, Hexham NE47 6NN
- **Cost**: Adults £9.60, Children £5.80.

- Vindolanda: Dig into the rich weave of Roman life at Vindolanda, a historical site filled with objects and insights into the daily routines of soldiers and citizens.

- **Address:** Bardon Mill, Hexham NE47 7JN
- **Cost**: Adults £7.50, Children £4.50.
- **Personal Experience:** Our journey along Hadrian's Wall submerged us in the sounds of ancient societies, while the digs at Vindolanda offered a fascinating glimpse into the lives of those who once walked these famous lands.

North York Moors: Rugged Beauty and Quaint Villages - Overview: Embark on a journey of natural discovery amidst the wild landscapes of the North York Moors, where heather-clad moors, quiet dales, and beautiful villages await.

 - **Highlights:**

- **Goathland:** Journey to the idyllic village of Goathland, set amidst rolling hills and green fields, and immerse yourself in the timeless charm of its rustic houses and wandering paths.

- **Personal Experience:** *Our stay in Goathland took us to a world of rural calm, where sheep grazed on green slopes and the sounds of village life echoed through the valley.*

Local Language and Phrases: *Talking Like a Local*

➢ **Greetings:**
- "**Hiya**" - Informal greeting equivalent to "*Hi*" or "*Hello.*"
- "**Howay**" - Expression of encouragement, similar to "*Come on*" or "*Let's go.*"

Local Phrases:

- **"Gan canny"** - *Take it easy or be careful.*
- **"Aye"** - *Yes.*
- **"Why aye, man"** - *Yes, of course.*

Food and Drink:
- **"Canny scran"** - *Good food.*
- **"Pint of broon ale"** - *A pint of brown ale, a popular local beer.*
- **"Bait"** - *A meal or snack, often used to refer to packed lunches for outdoor activities.*

Directions:
- **"Doon the road"** - *Down the road or street.*
- **"Ower yonder"** - *Over there, in the distance.*
- **"Gan up the toon"** - *Go into town or the city center.*

Local Sayings:

- "**How's yer father**?" - *How are you or how's it going?*

- "**Haddaway and shite**" - Expression of disbelief or dismissal, similar to "*Nonsense.*"

Polite Expressions:
- "**Cheers**" - *Thank you or goodbye.*
- "**Ta**" - *Thank you.*

Closing Remarks:
- "**Catch ya later**" - *See you later.*
- "**Have a gan**" - *Have a good time or enjoy yourself.*

These resources and phrases will enhance your experience in Northumberland and help you connect with locals while exploring the region's rich heritage and natural beauty. Whether seeking assistance, navigating the countryside, or engaging in friendly conversation, these tools will ensure a memorable and immersive journey through Northumberland's diverse landscapes and communities.

CONCLUSION

Your Northumberland Adventure Awaits

As we end this trip through the fascinating scenery, rich history, and lively culture of Northumberland, we invite you to start on your adventure and discover the wonders that await in this charming area. From the stately castles and old ruins to the rocky shore and beautiful towns, Northumberland offers a mix of experiences that will leave you spellbound.

As you cross the lively streets of Newcastle Upon Tyne, dive into the calm beauty of the countryside, and tour the secret gems tucked away in historic towns and villages, you'll find yourself submerged in a world where history comes to life and nature calls with its wild beauty.

Whether you're wanting love trips, family-friendly activities, or solo breaks amidst nature,

Northumberland has something to offer every tourist. Lose yourself in the timeless charm of its scenery, delight in the warmth of its welcome, and create memories that will last a lifetime.

So, pack your bags, lace up your boots, and get ready to start on an amazing journey through Northumberland. Your adventure awaits, and the wonders of this amazing area are yours to find. From the busy streets of Newcastle to the calm shores of Lindisfarne, let Northumberland's magic facinate your heart and soul. Bon voyage, and may your Northumberland trip be filled with joy, discovery, and endless wonder.

Thank you

Printed in Great Britain
by Amazon